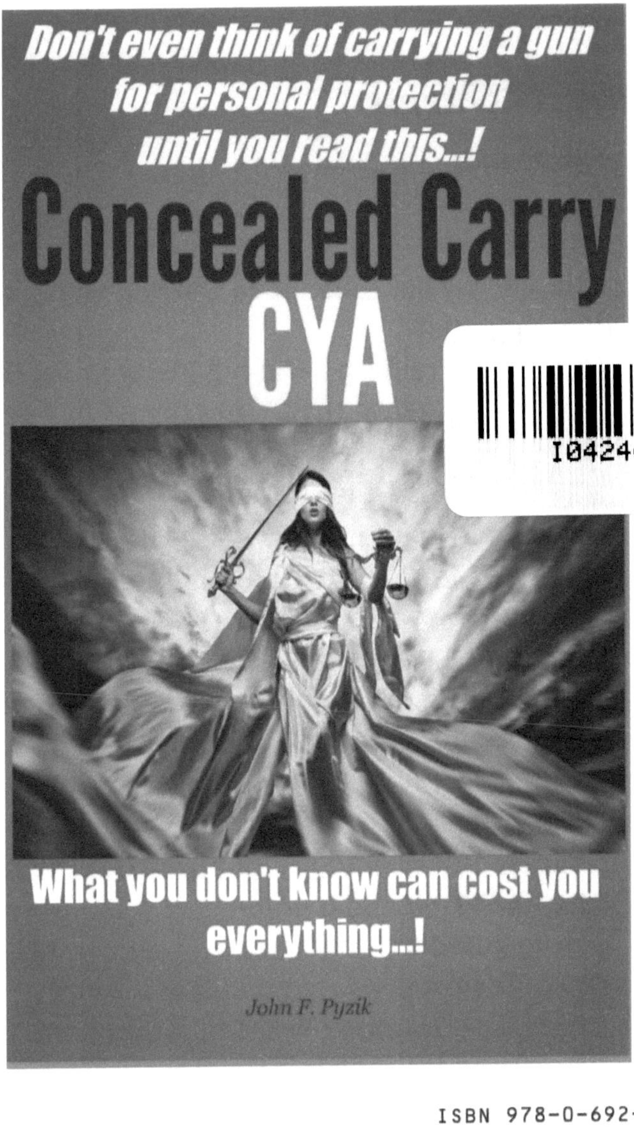

Don't even think of carrying a gun
for personal protection
until you read this...!

Concealed Carry
CYA

What you don't know can cost you
everything...!

John F. Pyzik

$17.97
ISBN 978-0-692-46920-0
51797>

9 780692 469200

1

Table of Contents

Disclaimer

The author of this book is not an attorney and does not offer legal advice in this book. You should always contact competent legal counsel for your individual situation. The content of this book is based upon my training and graduation from the Indiana Law Enforcement Academy, EMT Certification, many additional courses with veteran law enforcement instructors, the FBI and many miles of street-level knowledge and experience as a former police officer/chief. This book is intended to inform anyone planning on carrying a weapon for self-defense of the responsibilities, potential risks/liabilities, dangers, and consequences associated with a decision to carry a weapon.

Safety is the utmost factor when considering a firearm, and homes with children and young teenagers should always have secure provision to prevent inadvertent or immature access to any weapon. Part of that process is education and appropriate age-level communication with your children, plus locked, secure storage while you are not in direct and immediate control of their activities.

Children do not understand consequences associated with firearms and many teenagers are only aware of firearms from TV or video games. As you know, but they may not comprehend, there is no reset button with real firearms...just "game over" and they do not need to play that one. Parents must weigh the additional risks vs. benefit of possessing an in-home firearm when children/grandchildren/ teenagers are still living at your home or visiting. *(I cannot even begin to convey how heartbreaking the 40-minute ride was in the back of an ambulance, as we transferred a young teenager to an Indianapolis hospital for a self-inflicted bullet wound to his head. There was nothing we could really do for him after the bullet ripped through his right temple and tore through his brain. It was his last ride...to eternity...and I will never forget it...even decades years later. He just had no concept of consequences.)*

Foreword

Thank you for choosing this book to help you consider the major issues associated with owning and legally carrying a firearm for personal protection. You will find the content informative, insightful and blended with enough real-life, depictions and surreal-life examples of what can happen to an upstanding citizen who decides to carry gun to protect his life and his loved ones.

This book is not intended to scare you or discourage your from exercising your Constitutional right to legally own and carry a firearm for personal protection. However, real-life encounters can become very dangerous, and the breaking news reports remind us that not everyone out there is wonderful. In fact the level of violence is so reckless and growing, you have an even more serious family responsibility to protect yourself and your loved ones from it.

The scenarios and examples are provided to show why it is necessary in today's world to keep yourself and your family protected from attacks wherever they might occur: home, roadways, drug store, Wal-Mart, walking the dog, shopping malls, even at church. The threats are too serious and becoming more frequent and "closer to home" to ignore the greater consequences of becoming a helpless victim of violence, whether at the hands of local thugs or international terrorists.

The balance of your decision on whether to legally carry a firearm places survival on one side of the scale and risk/liability on the other. If it ever becomes necessary for a prosecutor, judge or jury to read the scale because of your involvement with a lethal incident, you want to be sure the scale clearly tilts in your favor... overwhelmingly.

To help ensure that you don't become a victim of your own survival response, you will certainly want to obtain qualified education, training, legal counsel and a written guidance/code of personal response to various potential situations.

Discussing the matter pro-actively with your attorney is one of the best ways to make sure that you understand the particulars of your laws and reduce the risks/liabilities associated with the use of lethal force for self-defense.

While no book, training or experience can prepare you for every real-life contingency, the value in ongoing training for that once-ever life challenge, will keep you more aware and focused to respond effectively, and more likely survive, prevail and continue a near-normal life afterwards. Your life is too important to leave this issue to default or random chance.

Introduction

Nightly news reports of violence in our streets scream outrage beyond any comprehension for the everyday citizen who goes to work or school or normal daily activities.

Major metros have "hidden" major crime statistics.

In Indianapolis, the murders-by-gun in recent years surpassed the American troop annual casualties during the Afghanistan war ...for the entire country.

The numbers don't lie. The politicians do.

In 2014, the crimes statistics for 9 out of the Top 10 deadliest cities in the US recorded more homicides in each city than the average annual US Troop hostile fire casualties in Afghanistan, the country.

U.S. Troops killed-in-action in Afghanistan (iCasualties.org):

Year	Total
2001	4
2002	20
2003	17
2004	24
2005	66
2006	65
2007	83
2008	133
2009	266
2010	440
2011	365
2012	246
2013	85
2014	25
Total	**1,839/14 years (131** average U.S. soldier casualties/year)

2014 Top-10 Deadliest US Cities by murders (The Daily Beast)

Chicago	407
New York	328
Detroit	304
Los Angeles	259
Philadelphia	248
Houston	239
Baltimore	217
New Orleans	150
Indianapolis	135
Dallas	111
Total	**2398 (Murders one year)**

American cities are more dangerous than a war zone...?

While none of these statistics can measure the violence and pain caused to the victims and their families, 9 of the top-10 deadliest US cities in the year 2014 recorded annual murder rates higher than the average annual troop casualty rate in the Afghanistan war zone for the 14 years of the war. In fact, the top-ten most deadly US cities recorded annual murder rates 18 times higher than the average annual US troop casualty rate in a declared war zone.

You were safer in Afghanistan than in a major mid-west city...really? While the Indianapolis tragedy is just one metropolitan crime story, headlines are the same or worse in any large metropolitan area, even more dramatic in Chicago, Detroit, Atlanta, Baltimore...Take your pick.

WHY?

The signs are everywhere.

The "Common Denominators" of violence are obvious.

The reasons are visible by day and night.

If you know where trouble is, don't go there...

The "common denominators" in every center of violence are universally documented and undeniable. Your survival plan is best stated in one word... avoidance. Stay away from the centers of violence, the darkness hours and the potential situations that are proven magnets for dangerous encounters. If you know where the bad things are happening, just don't go there, especially at night.

The numbers don't lie...but...

The suggestion that big cities are more dangerous than a recent war zone will obviously not be popular with any of the big-city mayors/politicians, but one simple rule, "avoid the trouble spots" will keep you away from the majority of potentially deadly encounters that we hear about daily on the news.

Even more shocking, the random acts of violence have spread beyond the "common denominator" demographics and have made their way into the most unlikely of places...sometimes even during church services. But you already know this and that is another reason why you are considering or have purchased a weapon and applied for a gun permit.

You can't stay away from "everywhere" to avoid violence.

Recently, a single mother in Indianapolis was attacked on her front porch by a vicious knife-wielding thug who scraped his weapon to her neck.

Unprepared to defend herself any other way, she offered her purse without struggle and "cut a deal" with the felon to let him have her money and everything else in the purse if he would just let her go. Fortunately, her words made it easy for him, and he felt that he did not need to kill to get what he wanted...but that is no guarantee of a future good outcome for similar situations.

Even "Home-Sweet-Home" isn't safe sometimes...

Since you can't stay away from your home, maybe sitting alone on your front porch at 3 A.M., deeply involved with one of your textbooks in preparation for your next class, is not the best way to avoid danger....

The first rule...avoid situations, places, people or events that historically fit the definition of high risk. That "rule" may even apply to your front porch at certain times.

If you have found yourself in a similar or an even less-violent incident, you feel violated and will vow to never again be caught in any type of a life-threatening situation without an adequate way to defend yourself.

14

How to protect your family and home from assault…

Millions of people have responded to fear for their safety...

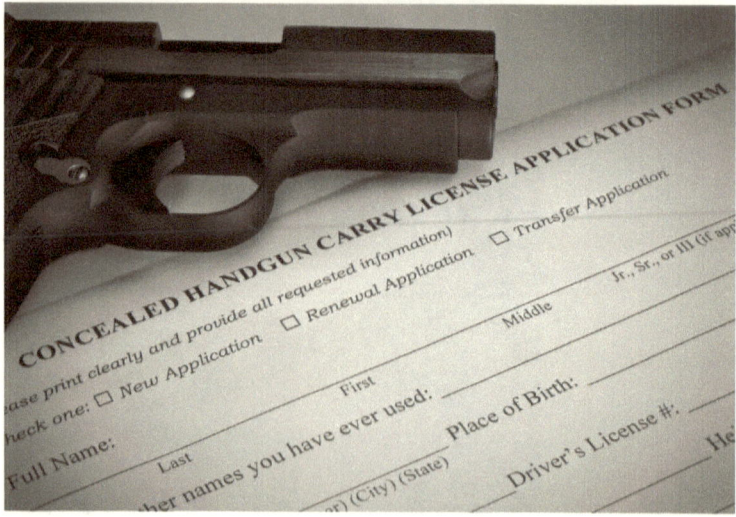

The typical response is to purchase a handgun, followed by a stash of ammunition, holsters, and an application for a personal protection permit, license, gun permit or whatever it is called in your state.

This process is very specific, requiring personal information, medical or mental health questions, fingerprints, and a registration fee and a witnessed application signature.

"I'm mad as hell, and I'm not going to take it anymore !"

Think again...

The major motivation for carrying a gun starts with a personal or friend/relative's close call or a news article or program that has heightened awareness, scared or terrified them.

Unfortunately, this is where the process stops for most people. Fortunately, you recognize that these are just the first steps in your personal protection plan and that there is much more you will consider and act upon before you accept the responsibility of carrying a firearm on your person. Don't even think of carrying a firearm until you read the next chapters.

Chapter 1-Your License to Carry a Gun...& the best way to not need it.

A state-issued gun permit is a license to carry a gun, not a license to kill someone who causes you some degree of danger in the future. Guns have no place in "settling arguments". The standard for self-defense is always based upon what a reasonable person would do when faced with an imminent, no-way-to-escape, life-threatening or serious bodily injury-level of danger by an armed or overwhelming assailant.

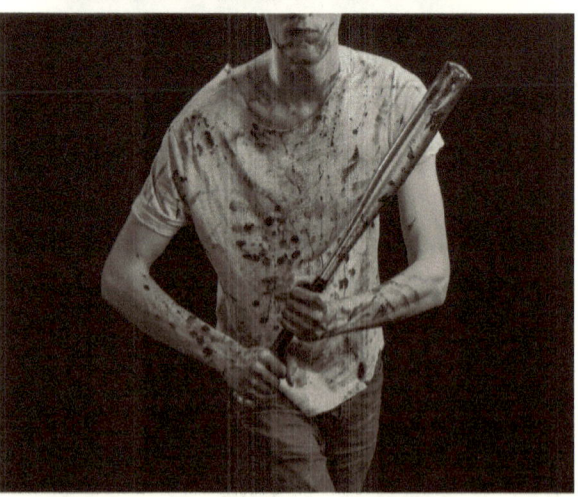

Life-threatening assaults can come your way in many different "formats"!

Sometimes imminent, deadly and unavoidable encounters are obvious, but...

...for the vast majority of other situations, a much more civilized solution is called for....Avoidance is the best choice, communication, agreement, leave, call police... anything other than using the gun...only as a last resort to address unavoidable, imminent, serious/violent/deadly, direct aggression to your person or someone else near you, where your defense actions would be considered reasonable, appropriate and proportional to the threat or demonstrated violence and prevent it from continuing.

However...

In almost all other situations, the reasonable, appropriate and proportional response by you would not involve a gun.

The Days of the Wild West are over...

Although the days of the Wild-West are officially gone in terms of self-defense for "honor's sake", the nightmares of violence are just as wild and as dangerous as they ever were, especially in the inner cities because there is no honor, respect, or morals with the gangs, drug cartels, drive-by-shooters and street thugs.

Just look at the street and what's out there...

The "career paths" of many youth are destined to a cell or a casket.

You don't want to go there with them or because of them...

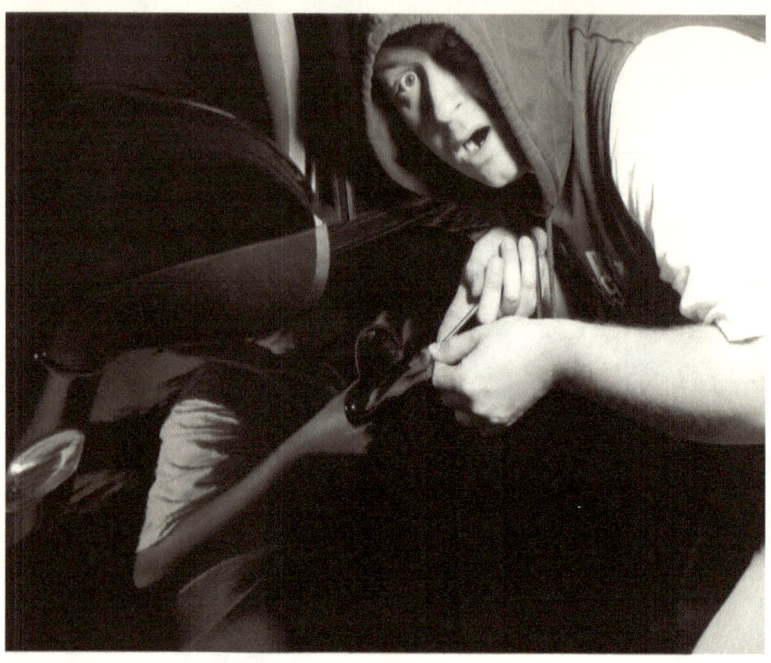

You don't want them taking you along for a "ride" on their journey…, that's why you applied for and received your permit…to legally carry a gun for personal protection for you and your family.

You can never know for sure, but you want to be ready for that one time an unforeseen, surprise, unavoidable, dangerous, violent, encounter with someone, pursuing an agenda that places you in a life-and-death situation. You just want to be ready and be able to defend your loved ones, others and/or yourself.

As a duty-bound citizen, your preparation should include ongoing training on how to safely use, store and carry your gun…only after you have been approved and licensed by your state and issued an official permit.

Note: it is probably a felony in your state to carry a handgun on your person or in your vehicle if you do not have the proper license. (If you just purchased the gun and do not have a permit to carry, have the receipt in your pocket, the unloaded gun in your trunk in a secure container, preferably locked and separated from the ammunition or if you have it similarly secured and on your way to hunting/target practice…with your appropriate gun license for sport or target practice in your possession.)

Chapter 2-Training...The big lie and how it can kill you.

Now that you have cleared the ownership and legal carry processes/permits, sign up for safety and target-practice lessons as the next steps to familiarize yourself with the gun, how to aim, fire, reload and group your shots in a pattern. While these are essential requirements for responsible gun ownership and personal protection carry, this training will in no way prepare you for the reality of a gun situation on the streets or against a violent home intruder.

Violent intruders don't play by any rules, but you have to.

It's all so easy and "programmed" on the training/target ranges.

If you have checked the YouTube "gun gurus videos" that demonstrate how to site your weapon, proper two-handed grip, defensive stance, controlled breathing, smooth trigger squeeze techniques, laser sights and bullet selection, you realize that there are a lot of "focused" gun people out there, spending much of their lives tweaking sights and polishing bullets, "totally prepared" for any assault on their person or property. Don't get obsessed with a lot of things that will not matter if you get into a gun-level encounter.

Certainly continuous training, preparation and practice are absolutely essential to optimize your survival chances in a life-threatening situation.

The one element that all the practice cannot duplicate is the reality-of-the-moment when an armed assailant attacks. Violence cannot be duplicated by training in any real measure. Only until you actually experience it, can you begin to understand how it shocks, overwhelms and "paralyzes" and totally consumes you in the moment.

When it comes your way, the attacker has already made up his mind what he is going to do to you, and the way he knows that he will overpower you is with the element of surprise and lightening-speed assault. That is how they prey on innocent victims and prevail even before you can even think about responding to defend yourself or stop the attack.

Trained & ready for anything….on the range.

Do you really believe that you will have time to find your gun, grip it with both hands, turn on the laser sight, flip the safety off, aim, hold your breath and return fire at a stationary attacker, who is posed for six seconds in one spot (just like the targets at the practice range) so that you can shoot him and end his career/life of crime? Unfortunately that is not how it plays out in reality.

The Big Lie

The "big lie" in much of the guru advice and target practice is that you probably will not have time to respond to the surprise attack, and if you can, you may very well be injured from the initial attack.

So, the two-handed grip training that you perfected at significant cost in time, ammo and range fees will be of little or no value. You may have a chance to get a random shot off in response, but even if your gun is perfectly "tuned in", polished and ready to go at a moment's notice, your moment has already passed...and so has the attacker. It's over in seconds...two-three for the initial attack...maybe five for the encounter and four seconds for the escape.

You can never be totally prepared for every attack, just trained to tilt the odds in your favor. Sometimes, even that will not help you. While driving home from work late one night on a major Indianapolis highway, the passenger side, front window exploded into thousands of pieces from a temporarily-deafening concussion caused by a sniper bullet grazing the safety glass.

I reported the incident to the local Sheriff's Department, but it was a dark night and the shot could have come from anywhere...from any distance...just one of three random victims of violence recorded that night by drivers in the same area.

Chapter 3-Reality 101...You only have 2 or 3 seconds...

Because this point is so key, it needs to be restated in real-life, to make sure you have some insight to the "reality of the street". Your gun will not help you in most instances, even one that has been "customized" and "certified" for accuracy, equipped with a laser sighting system and an instant-off safety.

It won't help in the majority of encounters *(It may even be used against you.)* and here is why. You are being watched. Aside from the "watching" that takes place for your own good via security cameras, security personnel, NSA, CIA, Google, Facebook, and a host of "harmless" watchers, the bad guys have you on "radar" before they spring into action.

You don't even know it, but "violence" is watching for opportunity.

The face of violence is as "cold" as the steel of the gun at your head.

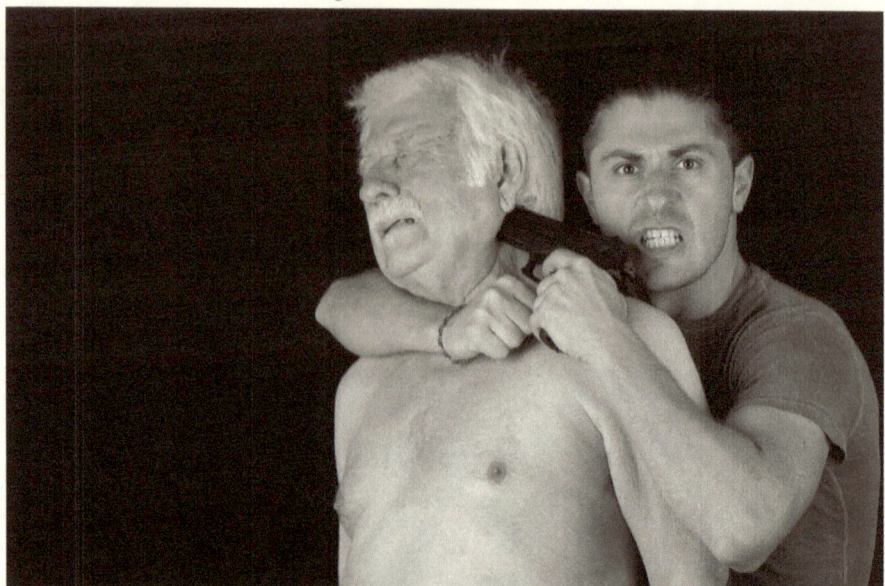

You won't have a clue its coming until you feel the cold steel of a semi-automatic pistol jammed against your head with some frantic, unintelligible, screaming that you know means, "Hand over your f_____ money ! and shut the f_____ up."

Crime statistics, newspaper articles and TV stories continually remind us of the growing threat levels, but the madness is academic until you see or feel it thrust upon you or your family. Denial and "It won't happen to me" mentalities just make it easier for criminals to show you how wrong you are.

Carrying a licensed self-protection weapon is no guarantee that you will survive, but not having a way to defend yourself is a tragedy in waiting.

None of the consequences and subsequent legal scenarios detailed in this book are intended to discourage the lawful and licensed carrying of a weapon to help deter violence against you or your family. To not protect yourself is a regret that you will never get over if life-threatening violence comes your way…at the store, jogging, even worshiping with your family.

No monument or parade will be scheduled for you if you do legally respond and save the day, but no monument or procession will be needed for you or your family either…just another example of reality recognized, responded to and prevailed against by you…Reality 101…Survival.

Premium weapon upgrades are nice, but not a guarantee of survival.

Sometimes your State permit, your reliable handgun, equipped with premium grips and all, but tucked in your concealed-carry, leather pocket holster will just be unavailable and a very poor option if you try to "go for it".

You have been had. Your best course may just be to go along with the attacker's instructions dutifully and hope that he leaves after he gets what he wants.

If he does, which is most of the time, you are the winner. You are alive, albeit a little poorer, but alive and will certainly be more cautious and aware of your surroundings in the future. The attacker is gone and probably doesn't even know who you are or is in any state to even remember or care. You were just easy prey…with money…and he got it.

You may have some instant decisions to make...

If he proceeds to physically attack you or demonstrates that he wants to add to your harm, then you have to measure your probability of successfully reaching for your gun and using it to prevent serious, unavoidable imminent danger or choosing to fight back some other way or run for cover. Although reaching for your gun is still no guarantee of survival, not reaching for it may in some cases be a certain outcome.

Because you do not know the ultimate intention of the attacker, you can only assume by his assault upon you with a directed handgun, that he is willing to and may kill you. At that point your choices and outcomes are extremely limited, and no one can tell you the best way to deal with the total madness of the moment. **The "blur of the moment" may work for or against you...**

Violence is processed by the human mind a number of ways...often in "slow motion" a "total freeze" or a kaleidoscope of images, maybe even focus-fade for a second.

A moving, racing, running target can easily get lost in the blur of the emotion and adrenalin, especially one that is darting, side-to-side or fading in the distance or

30

dark, disappearing out of sight at full run or acceleration…certainly, not a Saturday-morning practice-range target. However, if you chose to run from the assault and if the attacker shoots at you while you are trying to get away, you have a chance that he will miss because he is also in an agitated state and a fraction of an inch off-target at the barrel end is several feet off-target the longer the distance from the gun.

Certainly, you are not choosing among any good options, but anything is better than sitting there and taking a bullet to the head. There is no absolute rule on how to best handle hypothetical situations, but you just have to weigh your options and risks and try what you think is best for the moment and circumstance.

Chapter 4-Two-three seconds is all you have...

After graduating from the Indiana Law Enforcement Academy and attending many supplemental training courses with the FBI and other agencies and serving on the Madison County Sheriff's Department as reserve officer before becoming a fulltime police officer and subsequently, the police chief of a small town, I can tell you from first-hand experience that you only have one-two, maybe three seconds to respond to a life-threatening situation with your personal protection handgun.

After that point, you might have to deal with a surprise attack some other way, talking, hand-to-hand combat, pipe, bat, whatever else you can grab or run, take cover, pull away or fight and hope that your training and luck will enable you to survive.

Chapter 5-Real-Life Story #1

One time, after my police officer days, I did not have a weapon when a very agitated factory employee, much larger than me, grabbed a fire-axe off the safety station and started towards me. He wasn't mad at me…just mad at the system and supervision.

Mad at the world and someone was going to get the "axe".

I looked him in the eye, forced a tight smile and just said, "Hey put that down before somebody gets hurt!" He thought about it for a second and realized his best long-term option was to put it back where he got it…I could just see the forces of reason overrule his temporary urge to fix the problem with a four-foot-long fire axe. Sometimes, words are the best defense, and sometimes they aggravate the issue. When you have no other options, words can work wonders in a potentially lethal situation.

Chapter 6-Real-Life Story #2

Another time, I was the one with the "surprise" for three armed robbers who had just "knocked off" a gas station and were trying to get out of town. I monitored the dispatch on my walkie-talkie with the vehicle description and license number of the getaway car, containing the three robbers as they raced away from the scene, my direction.

I had just sat down at the truck stop and placed a "lunch" order just after midnight because I was working third shift that day and already put a few miles on the road. According to the Madison County Sheriff's Department dispatch, the robbers were last seen leaving a nearby town on a state highway that led through the same area as the restaurant. I quickly explained to the waitress that I had to leave to answer a call and headed to a lookout road that intersected the projected robbers' path.

The road was dark and empty from the one direction, but then…

Within three or four minutes of my arrival at the intersection in my unmarked Plymouth Fury, the car described in the dispatch raced by, but then it began to gradually slow down and pull over to the roadside, about a quarter mile past the intersection. I later learned that the robbers were confused about which road would lead them back to Indianapolis.

I turned right out of my observation spot, no red lights or siren, and cautiously pulled up behind the already-stopped getaway car with three occupants, the number that also matched the original broadcast. After the dispatcher confirmed the car description and license number as the one involved in the robbery a few minutes ago, I calmly reminded myself that I was outnumbered, and the only chance I had for getting these guys, was surprise.

A "plain-no-markings Plymouth, "paid for itself" that night.

There was just something about my plain-looking, unmarked Plymouth that night that did not arouse their suspicion enough to again reach for their shotgun from the robbery.

I inched up slowly behind them, stopped, got out of my car and walked casually up to the driver's side door with the pre-jacked 12-gauge Mossberg dangling parallel to my right leg until I reached his open window. *(Maybe, it was luck and the coincidence that my duty jacket had just come back from the cleaners and the chrome badge had not been replaced on the left breast pocket yet. Probably, both factors worked to my survival that night.)*

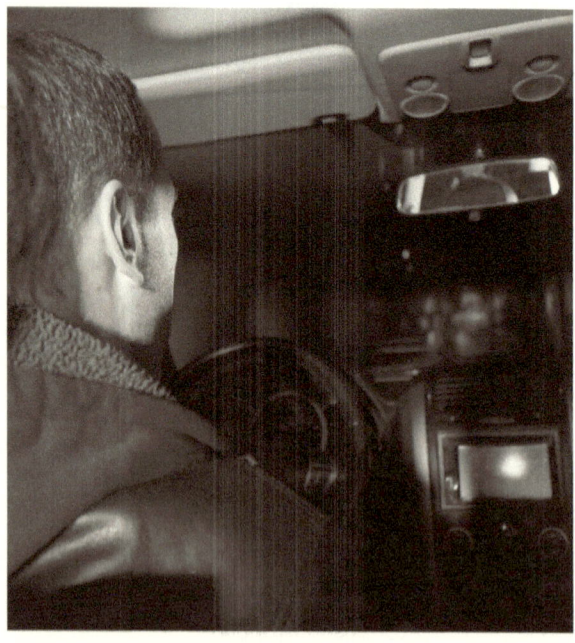

The robbers may have suspected something, but not the police.

I saw them looking behind, but they couldn't see me because of my headlights, and they didn't get any time to figure it out because it all happened so quickly.

The police surprise measured 12 Gauge...and spoke their language...

The robbery and get-a-way came to a "no contest" sudden end!

Rage. Shock. Terror...they were all there in the driver's face which turned immediately red-then-pale-ashen when I jammed the barrel of the 12 gauge shotgun through the open window and ordered all three out of the car with the exact words I have long-since forgotten. There was no argument, no fuss, just the most nervous compliance I have ever seen. Why...because of the surprise and the overwhelming possibility that none in their car would survive a round of double-00 buckshot from the "cannon" pointed at them.

Surprise, caution, luck, Providence...all put survival & capture on the side of the law...

Fortunately, the illegal sawed-off shotgun they had used in the robbery was not waiting for me at the driver's window when I walked up to greet them and fortunately for them that they all "behaved nicely" with their hands on the trunk of the getaway car and their legs spread...until seven additional backup officers arrived to cuff and transport them back for positive ID and a trip to jail.

Each received a new "portrait" and Identity number:

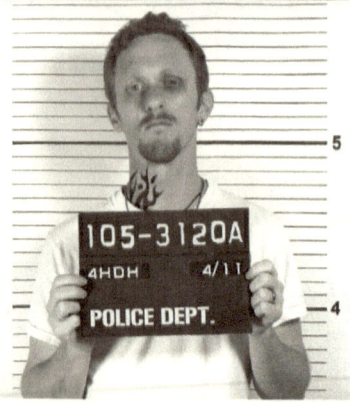

...and a chance to tell their side of the story...silence.

Even though they were dangerously armed and outnumbered me, three-to-one, I had the element of surprise and a weapon that overwhelmed them...for a good cause that time and introduced them a new definition for the term "bars".

On the other side of the law, criminals use the element of surprise and your low awareness of lurking telltale signals going on around you. These factors enable attackers to use your distractions against you...often to tragic end. Stay alert, aware and remember the corollary to Murphy's law that someone relayed to me many years ago and has served me well since: *"Murphy was an optimist."*

Just remember, you may have two-three seconds, at the most, to make a forever decision and there is a real probability one of your hands/arm may be engaged in self-defense with the attacker or disabled from the initial attack.

The attacker hasn't been advised that you possess a $500-$1,000 semi-auto with precisely-"tuned" laser sites, loaded with high-performance bullets in one of the best double action pistols, equipped with a quick-flip, thumb safety, ready-and-waiting for deployment by a range-trained, two-handed stance shooter who can place a five-inch pattern on a stationary target at 15 yards in 20 seconds (with hearing protection), after careful, non-stressed, 4-second aiming for each shot in daylight conditions.

None of that matters when his gun is on you. Vigilance, awareness and caution are your best self-defenses. Avoid the obvious geography and conditions that historically have "generated" confrontations that never have good outcomes. You don't want to "win" a fight with your gun. You don't want to have the fight that will cost you everything for the rest of your life...if you survive the moment.

Chapter 7-L.A.P.D. sent Smith & Wesson back to drawing board.

Do you see how the reality of the encounter might not match the "Preparations"? There is a key reason, other than price, that the L.A. Police Department advised Smith & Wesson that the police department was not interested in their off-the-shelf, Bodyguard .380 (left) with its finger-activated, laser sights for their officers' backup weapons…

In addition to price, that feature contributed no value in a last-ditch struggle for survival when an officer's primary gun is disabled, empty or pulled by the criminal/attacker.

At that point, the situation is body-to-body battle that calls for the simplest, most reliable and quickly deployable weapon…one where Murphy's Law has been minimized in favor of the officer…no switch-on laser…safety off...nothing but a quick trigger pull to change the outcome. (Laser sights are a great advantage at distance, but switch-activated ones require time and another "step" in the self-defense reaction. Even though the laser does not have to be on for the gun to fire, it is a potential programmed distraction which tilts the scale against your survivability in a hand-to-hand battle for control of an officer's gun.)

Some new semi-automatics are just "pull & shoot"…no external safety switches.

Kahr CW9

The new brand-name, semi-automatic, handguns (Kahr CW9) come without an external safety switch…? While your initial reaction to the "no safety switch" may be negative, you have to determine if you will have the presence of mind in a life-threatening attack to remember to deal with turning the safety switch off when directly confronted by an armed attacker.

Once again, maybe the best thing to do is just hand over your wallet or money without a struggle or weapon use on your part…especially if the attacker appears to only be interested in the money and you couldn't get to your weapon quickly.

If you are convinced that the attacker is about to deal you catastrophic harm and if you have no other way out, you will want the simplest, easiest-to-use, no-frills, no switches handgun that you can get…with one hand…either hand…trigger-pull only. Kahr CW9 works same, either hand, both hands, no switches…just quick, reliable protection.

Most premium hand guns also have many built-in internal safety features to reduce accidental discharge, including double action mechanisms and firing pin interlocks that only "activate" when the trigger is squeezed all the way back to a predetermined position.

Other larger semi-automatic hand guns also have thumb-lever and/or grip safety releases too, but these are primarily open-carry side-arms, intended for badged professionals who wear them while on duty, are regularly trained and have graduated from the police academy.

These officers know their weapons and how to use them instinctively…Civilians generally just don't have that same open-carry need, level of skill, training or practice time to carry one of these guns around with daily dress/attire.

When faced with the imminent danger of losing your life to an assailant, you will want a pull-the-trigger-only, one-handed, without a side-button, laser activation or safety deactivation, reliable gun that does what it is supposed to and stop the life-threatening attack because you will not have the option of a "replay".

This is one reason why the revolver remains a very popular option. It is just, pull, point and shoot…simple, reliable and effective if you think five or six rounds will be enough to do the job…which it is statistically.

Chapter 8-Gun in your face...What should you do?

You are more likely to pull into your garage, turn the engine off, step one foot out of the door and look up to a "45" or a "9" staring you in the face.

At that point, you have some decisions to make...Again, maybe, the better course of discretion doesn't include a reach for your gun at that moment. Maybe, humble acquiescence and a property-loss insurance claim are better ways to deal with the issue. You have to judge, pick your response and hope you get it right in one or two seconds.

This type of situation underscores the value of hand-to-hand self-defense training along with your range training, if you are physically able.

Notwithstanding the gun-in-your-face encounter, in almost every other type of threatening situation I encountered as a police officer, there were alternatives which included communication, physical restraint, non-lethal weapons and, as an absolute last resort, the gun.

These scenarios underscore the need to train for reality, not for trophies or the highest range score if you are there for self-defense. Reality means single-hand, each-hand training, shooting, proficiency...right and left...both...!

Train with each hand, both hands. One may be injured in an attack.

Unless your gun is a revolver or a semi-automatic with thumb safety releases on both sides or a no-external safety semi-automatic, you cannot train effectively for one-handed shooting…which is street (survival) reality.

Chapter 9-Pick the right gun/caliber or suffer the consequences.

Caliber selection starts with the minimum. 9 mm (Glock-top) is the minimum caliber for semi-automatics and 38 caliber special (Smith & Wesson-bottom) for revolvers.

Longer cartridge contains more gunpowder and generates more stopping power.

These two are minimum acceptable calibers for self-defense. Others will argue that the .380 is virtually the same diameter, but it just does not have the punch as a primary defense weapon cartridge of 9 mm or the 38 because the shorter casing is packed with less powder and lighter bullets.

9 mm vs. .380 Cartridge

Advocates for the "mouse guns" will say that the .380 is O.K. as the minimum self-defense weapon, but I will guarantee you that you will be outgunned by the attacker. Even the 9 mm option will probably not stop an aggressor with just one shot, unless it hits center chest or the head.

Guns intended for a military holster are a challenge for concealed carry.

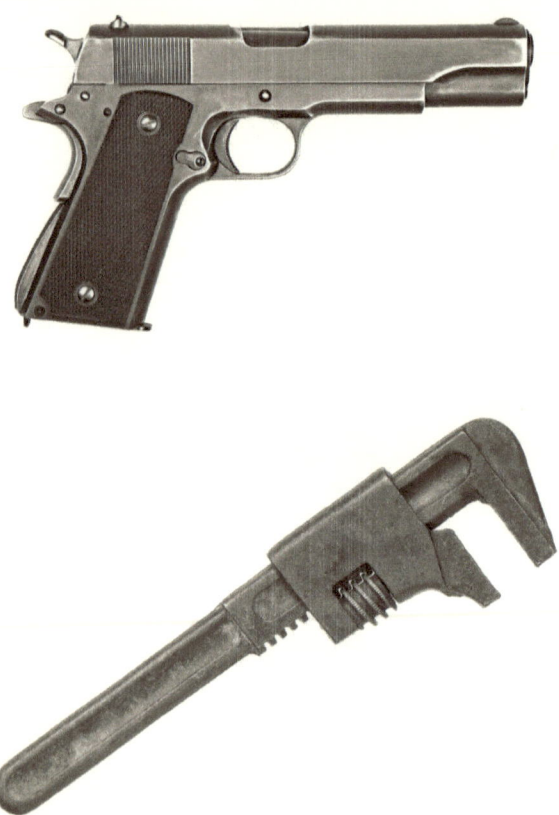

The old government model Colt 45 caliber single-action semi-automatic will knock an attacker backwards with one shot.

However, the gun is as big as a monkey wrench and may be more than most people would like to shoot, plus it is carried in a cocked position with two primary safeties, a back-of-the-handle squeeze grip and right-thumb tab to help prevent unintended discharge. Although, there is a Combat Model version with a shorter barrel and overall size, it still may be more than you want to lug around.

Guns that can fix the problem and create a bigger one…

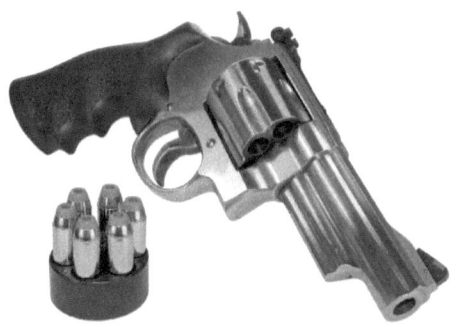

We carried Smith & Wesson Model 66 stainless steel .357 magnums on the sheriff's and at the police departments. Rounds 1, 3, 4, 5 & 6 were hollow points. The second round was an armor-piercing solid point, capable of disabling a car engine if necessary. Obviously way too much power for most urban situations, the gun was a cannon. It has been replaced in most areas by some version of a military semi-automatic or Glock 9 mm which holds more than double the number of rounds…although not nearly as powerful.

In the movie, *Dirty Harry*, Clint Eastwood packs a six-inch, 44 magnum as a plainclothes detective. Unless you are a very well-conditioned large man over 200 pounds in weight, and living in a jungle, I would not even think of such a weapon. You will certainly stop a violent aggressor with it…and the bullet will still have enough energy to go through a few walls and a couple of innocent bystanders…never for self-protection…maybe for bear hunting as a back-up to your primary hunting rifle, but not in a community.

In fact, the .357 magnum revolvers with a hot load will numb your hand after firing just a few target rounds, not to mention blowing your eardrums out from the blast concussion if you are not wearing ear protection. (My ears are still ringing after many years since last range-firing the S&W Model 66-.357 magnum.) It was a good idea to generally replace them in today's police holsters.

The FBI even felt that the 40 caliber automatics were just a little too hot to handle for agents, who spend most of their days at the desk, investigating paper and computer trails of criminals.

Although the 9 mm is not a one-shot man stopper in most situations, at least you can hold onto it, manage the recoil and place a second shot if necessary without suffering blast trauma from firing it.

Chapter 10-Select the right holster.

Select a holster that is made for and recognizes/fits your brand/caliber and model firearm and protects the trigger from any unintended movement during drawing, re-holstering and continuous carry. If you stick with the name-brand holsters that clearly state which models they are designed for, you will be good.

Since you only have seconds to react, which (concealed-carry) holster is best? It depends on your age, size, mobility, training, and type of clothing you wear in the seasons.

As a police officer, I carried two guns in the summer, three in the winter, plus a shotgun and 45 caliber, 30-shot "Thompson" semi-automatic under the front seat of my patrol car, which is far more than called for by civilians. Common sense and good judgment are key factors for sensible concealed carry.

Potential scenarios and responses are part of daily reminders to yourself as part of your heightened awareness self-training. What's going on around you, inside the building and outside any windowed public place, even your home are key elements of your necessary caution and readiness for whatever potential threats may be emerging or escalating. Awareness, not obsession is the right perspective.

Molded Kydex, belt-mounted, holster

Safe-carry and quick access are the most important considerations.

Inside-the-belt holster

Shoulder holster

When you shop for a holster, your goal is to select one that will give you quick access for the best chance to survive within the 2-3 second window of response time if you encounter a life-threatening event. Although I have tried every variation, there are tradeoffs for each one. If you want the best response time options, the belt mounted, opposite your primary shooting hand, with gun butt forward or the shoulder harness, inverted holster, opposite your primary shooting hand with gun facing back. The tradeoff is that you always have to wear a jacket or sport coat, but the major advantage is that you can get to the gun with either hand easily and in a grip position to fire. Every other holster arrangement limits you to just the primary-hand access or straps an uncomfortable "lump" to your belt.

Summer Carry Holster

Even though it is not an ideal way to carry, in the summer, I use a soft-fabric holster in my right front pants pocket. Tradeoff is that you have to wear loose dress-style pants, but you can discretely carry a 9 mm Ruger LC9 or similar, the minimum-caliber, defense protection without pocket printing the gun. One-hand access is very easy, but that's the good and bad news…concealed, but only accessible by one hand.

Chapter 11-Don't buy your next gun until you know these terms.

Double-action mechanisms refer to the process of the trigger pull that cocks and fires the round. Single action refers to mechanism of firing the round that has been pre-loaded and cocked or auto-loaded by a prior shot that jacks the slide back, clearing the spent casing and pushing the new bullet into the firing chamber. The finger force for the double action guns is generally greater than for a single action version and the trigger travel distance is usually much farther for double-action guns whether revolvers or semi-automatics.

Certain semi-automatic guns are fired in single-action mode, like the .45 automatic on the left. Revolvers may be fired by the double action method or by the single action method. If you manually cock the gun by pulling the hammer back and then pull the trigger each time, you will fire the gun by the single-action trigger-pull method. If you just pull the trigger back the full distance, you will fire the gun by the double-action method.

Semi-automatic pistols can be total double action (left), single-action only (top) double action for the first shot and then single-action for the remaining ones (bottom), requiring the first round to be fired by pulling the trigger all the way back and the remaining cartridges/bullets would be fired by just pulling the short-distance trigger pull, single action.

Obviously, the single action mechanism is the fastest firing, followed by the double-action/single action and finally the slowest method via the totally double action guns that require a near-full-length trigger pull for each shot.

Why should you care about single action (SA), single action/double (SA/DA), double action (DA)?

It is all about a fraction of a second advantage to respond and what you feel comfortable with for your defense weapon of choice. Here is what else you should know before making a trip to the gun store for explanation.

Virtually all revolvers do not have external safety mechanisms, even though most brand-name guns do have some internal safety features that prevent the gun from going off if it is dropped or bumped. As double action (DA) or single shot/single action mechanisms, the safety of these guns lies in the hand of the beholder and their reliability is virtually 100%. If one cartridge/bullet fails to fire or is defective, another trigger pull will rotate the cylinder to the next round.

Semi-automatic pistols can be utilize DA, SA or DA/SA mechanisms. Some DAs will not have external safeties, but virtually all SA or DA/SAs will have an external safety or two. If they don't, the gun is probably a foreign-made WW II relic and should be avoided and replaced with a new gun.

The rationale for no external safety for the DA is that their trigger mechanism requires a near full pull every time a shot is fired, just like revolvers. Semiautomatic pistols are generally more compact than revolvers, hold more rounds and are capable of firing much faster if you select a SA or DA/SA mechanism.

If you experience a cartridge mis-feed while attempting to fire the weapon, you will have to manually pull the slide back to eject the non-firing cartridge and let the slide snap forward to feed another bullet into the firing chamber.

Obviously, this will require your other hand, which may not be available in the situation. While semi-automatics are very reliable, mis-feeds occur occasionally and the consequences could be dire.

Many people prefer the revolver, even with its limited capacity and relatively slow repeat fire time, because of the "for sure" factor of the name brand manufacturers. Others prefer the benefit of having double capacity (12-17) for the number of bullets available to fire at a threat, a clear advantage of the double-stack magazine in the larger semi-automatic side arms, carried by the police and military.

Most police departments have now toned-down calibers from the .357 magnum revolvers to 9 mm handguns in semi-automatic configuration because they have confidence in their reliability. Double+ the available bullets to shoot is more important than the possibility of a rare mis-feed from a quality semi-automatic firearm.

After you have determined which type of gun and trigger action you prefer, wait for your previously-applied-for personal protection permit, issued by your state of legal residence to arrive. *Just applying for a permit, does not allow you to legally carry a gun. You must have the State-issued permit on your person also.*

After you have fully familiarized yourself with all the features and functionality of your weapon and have completed a certified safety training and target/range course, you may think you are ready to pack on your gun, head out the door, confident that you are prepared to protect yourself and your family from any life-threatening attacker...There are a couple of more major considerations.

Chapter 12-Laser sight for sure...Get the right one !

Although side-mounted laser button sights are not much use as back-up weapons for police to carry in case their primary sidearm is lost, disabled or removed in a hand-to-hand battle with a desperate criminal, an automatically-activated laser sight, either included as a back-grip button on certain Smith & Wesson semiautomatics or added as an aftermarket option, is a most valuable component of a daily-worn concealed-carry weapon.

If your new gun does not come with a passively activated grip laser, just confirm that you can buy an easily fitted match for your model. Several gun and accessory manufacturers offer laser sights that are side-button-switch activated, but I only know of a few current manufacturers, Crimson Trace and ArmaLaser that feature grip activation models which turn the laser beam on when you grasp the gun. Viridian makes a green laser that also has an automatic-on version when you draw it from their companion holster and LaserMax has a guide-rod laser...add on features that can tab out at $100-$300+.

Taurus with Crimson Trace (grip-activated button) Laser & Pocket Holster

The laser beam points where the potential bullet is targeted and brilliantly lights up a red dot on the destination. The aftermarket kits come with easy-to-install directions and take only about 10-minutes to attach. You will want to adjust them into alignment with your barrel sights at the firing range. An adjustment tool is provided, but mine was close enough, right out of the box, that I am very comfortable with its alignment.

Laser sights place the bright dot right on the target where the gun is pointed.

The red-dot laser feature alone may be enough to deter an active attacker, but if it doesn't you have a better chance of responding with an effective defense.

You will hear the old argument that the laser dot cannot be seen or is not effective in the bright daylight, but it at least will give you an aiming advantage at night and low-light encounters, which are probably more than 50% of the time...still a strong reason to have an automatically activated laser sighting system. You just will not have time or the presence of mind to find the switch/button on a manually activated laser sight in many instances. Remember, you only have a couple of seconds, at best, to respond to a potential deadly attack against you.

While nothing can predict how a real-life encounter will unfold, you can develop, with the counsel of your attorney, a set of rules on how and when you will react with your firearm. Almost always, the gun is the wrong choice, but write down in detail and memorize the situations when you would use your gun justifiably for your protection or for someone else, based on what you know, what you will next read about in this book and by discussing the matter with your attorney before you even think about carrying your gun.

Remember, you have a license to carry a gun. That is all. In essence, you have a license to protect yourself in a life-threating, imminent danger, no-other-way-out situation and in so doing, will introduce yourself to a whole host of personal potential liabilities, expenses, criticism, abuse, danger, harassment and even possible punishment, including jail time, judgments…more than you can imagine.

It's still better than being dead, but here are a few small examples of what you can expect if you ever have to use your weapon to protect yourself or your family from vicious, violent and imminent deadly attacker(s).

While you may think these scenarios are re-runs, you will thank me many times over…because if you read about them, you may help yourself avoid/handle them in life.

Chapter 14-Are you prepared at home?

If you are in your home when a violent, "door-busting", armed intruder makes his way in and aggressively tries to attack you or a member of your family, you determine that there is no other way to stop the impending violence, you shoot/kill the intruder and immediately call the police and emergency aid. You and your family will be questioned by the police. Call your attorney immediately.

You will probably have to hand your gun over to the police for the investigation/ evidence and processing. You will have to go to the police station for a follow up session, paperwork and photo, processing, etc.

When your family witness statements match yours and the shooting appears to be justified, you probably will not be detained or jailed, but the file will be turned over to the local prosecutor for review and a decision on whether to charge you with a crime.

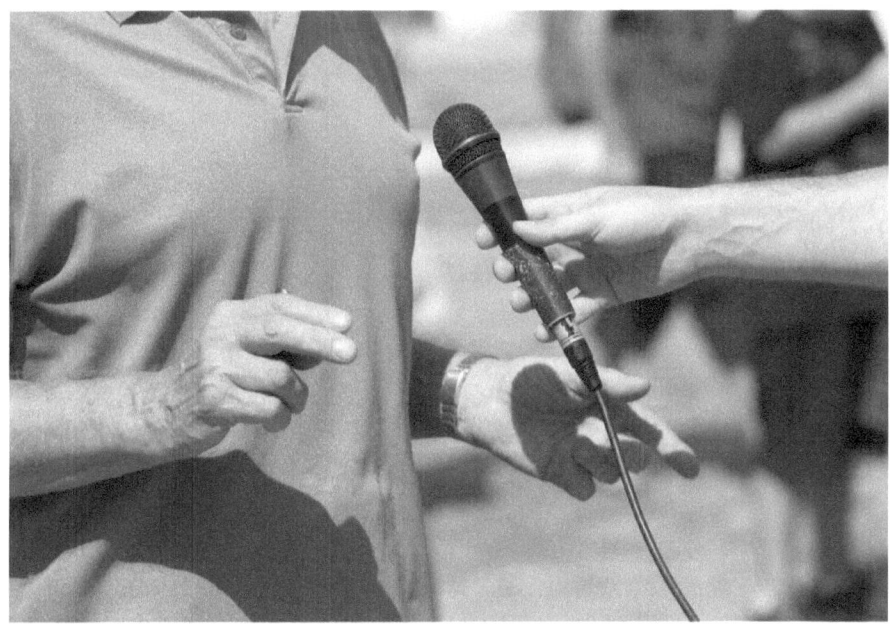

You will have the opportunity, many times, to address the media and have your face and story all over the local news…many times.

That consequence will make you very known to well-wishers, supporters, as well as the assailant's family/cohorts/partners-in-crime, who will harbor a great deal of animosity, rage and revenge because you "over-reacted" to an "innocent mistake" by their family member, and they will claim that he was just trying to get someone to help him with a flat tire….after all that's why he had the tire tool in his hand…wasn't it?

You are probably justified under the "fear for your life" reason, but historically, the family of the intruder will try to claim that the "poor child" (18-26 years old and living at home) was confused because of medication, lack thereof or because he was over-served alcoholic beverages or marijuana by some unscrupulous person at the strip bar he mistook for a church during the previous five hours.

If you think this all sounds ridiculous, just watch the nightly news or the COPS TV program or one of the "Court TV" series. It is always the fault of someone else when a young family member gets in trouble. ..And there is a whole phone book of Yellow-Pages-lawyers who will gladly take on a case to "right-some-evil" that has been inflicted upon their client…until the retainer fee is used up.

You may even prevail if a civil suit gets to court and you were justified under the particular circumstances of an imminent attack associated with a criminal charge against you, but your lawyer will be the real winner when your legal defense check clears.

So, you were 100% justified in defending your life and property while in your own home. That would be great if it were the end of the story.

However, just because you "won" the fight for survival and the legal challenges, family members of the thug who broke into your home and threatened your life most likely carry a "similar gene" for violence, get even or "transactional pay back" or dispensing the "unexplained accidents" that may occur on your residence, place of work, family, vehicle or other property…and that's if they get your address correct after they follow you home and then tell seven of their dudes that you live in the fifth house on the left side of "Elm Street" or was it the sixth house…?

Or your residence location was relayed through several "intermediaries" who ultimately pay a visit to the fourth house on "Elm Street" because they were on marijuana or wine when they heard where you lived. Either way, when the "even-the-score" visits or drive-bys occur, your neighbors will assume that the mistaken address attack was directed at you because they really have no enemies.

Note: Just because you find someone aimlessly wandering in your house and he is posing no immediate threat or appears to be confused, accidentally entered, under the influence of drugs, alcohol, medicine or a medical, dementia or other non-threatening condition, use of deadly force may very well be ruled as unjustified…in which case you may get jail time…Discretion and a reasonable response are always the standards by which your response will be judged.

Coincidental unexplained "accidents" are part of the pay back.

You probably will not be able to catch the culprits, because "nobody knows nothing".

These same neighbors are not really going to invite you to the next block party and will readily send you a bill for the broken glass from the rock that went through their picture window or the fire in their garage or their sliced tires. Whatever future crimes occur within 10 adjacent homes, it will get blamed on you for shooting somebody in this quiet neighborhood.

You may want to…or have to sell your home and move away.

(Hopefully not at a big discount for a quick sale.)

Unfortunately, as you have seen many times on TV recently, mob rule doesn't play by any rules or logic or facts, and you will have to cope with it.

If you are lucky, you can sell your house, but placing a "For Sale" sign out in front will just "open the door" to the realtor listing process which displays your floorplan, a phone number for a personal showing and open houses (open to anyone).

None of these factors will address your immediate safety concerns or your personal need to get out of the area without additional property damage from "certain relatives" of the thug, the ones with lots of memory, baggage and attitude still smoldering for the "unnecessary" loss of their dear loved one, who just happened to be in the wrong place at the wrong time…But you survived and are still alive.

If you think this is exaggeration, the next chapter is another page of the Reality 101 book.

Chapter 15-Another Real-Life Story?

Our police department had intercepted a relatively small marijuana stash ($50,000 street value) on the riverbank, before it was to be picked up by the intended receiver/distributor. As with most similar situations, we anticipated a "reaction" and transported the stash for safekeeping to the Anderson Police Department property vault. That night the windows were blown out of our police department headquarters in a drive-by retaliation by the "distributor." We never caught the "distributor," but I'm sure someone in the supply chain paid dearly for losing the $50K of "inventory".

Windows blown out of Police Department in a drive by as retaliation for intercepting drug drop.

Chapter 16-What if you are at the gas station and...?

The story is totally different if a similar encounter happens outside your locked door home. If you find yourself needing gasoline for your car after dark in the wrong place, you could very likely be faced with a hoodie-clad "visitor" who will demand your money and/or your car at the point of a gun, knife or other lethal weapons.

Usually, the best thing you can do is to give him what he wants and report the assault and robbery to the police after he has left, and you have carefully noted his description, recalled the license plate number and the direction of escape. That is the best response for such an encounter.

If the threat to your life cannot be avoided by any other means, and you are forced to respond, as a last resort, with your legally possessed and carried firearm, you may be fortunate enough in the one or two seconds you have to react to stop the immediate threat by shooting the attacker.

Your revolver and quick response to the highly-drugged attacker let you win.

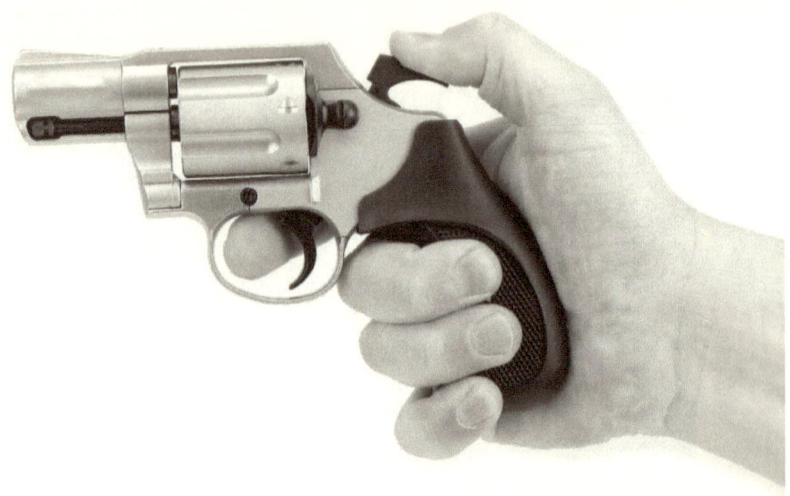

But what about the any background accomplice…who may also have a gun? He will either choose to run, give up or fight you for your weapon or shoot you too. If he runs, you were lucky again.

The immediate crime scene can get worse with every second...

In the highly unlikely event that he gives up, surrenders, or raises his hands, you have to figure how to summon reinforcements/police and deal with the chaos and hysteria at the scene. Since you are reluctant re-use your gun or too shocked or stressed out to shoot again, don't be surprised if at least one of the assailant(s) or someone from the bystander crowd picks up the downed robber's gun and runs off into the night.

By now the police have been summoned, sirens are wailing in the distance, the crowd is getting larger, the person shot is bleeding or dead on the ground and you are the only one standing there, holding a gun when the police show up.

Guess who gets another gun in the face....this time from the police who are dutifully responding to a number of cell phone calls with various descriptions of what just happened? Reality is, you are the only one at the scene with the incident weapon that was used on the bleeding/dead person on the ground.

The ambulance will take "forever" to arrive…maybe 5 to 10 minutes.

Late arriving bystanders will be screaming for your "hide" and hysterical relatives of the "alleged robber" will contribute to the chant for your demise in some vocabulary you may not have experienced recently.

The police are assigned to secure the scene from additional lethal events, assure aid/attend to the injured/deceased person and find out what happened. Since you are the one with the gun, you try to explain what happened, but are so overwhelmed by the tragedy and the new set of applied handcuffs and full-body frisk and pockets search that you have a difficult time being heard over the "calls for your head" by the growing crowd of clueless neighbors or drive-bys that want to see what is going on.

The police place you in the back of a squad car, hands still handcuffed, while waiting for the ambulance/coroner/ detectives to arrive. You are throwing up, have "wet" your pants or worse and are panic stricken by the confines of the police car, angry mob, flashing lights, sirens and the horror of what you just experienced…but that is just the beginning.

One of the back-up officers or detectives will come over to the police car you are seated in and read you your Miranda Rights, which is a brief warning that you have seen in the movies: "…anything you say can and will be used against you in a court of law….Do you understand your rights? Do you have any questions about what was just read you…?"

Then, you will be asked to describe what happened, followed by a series of follow-up questions…in particular, "Why did you shoot an 'unarmed' man?" At that point, you know the tide is not going your way, and you need some big-time help. If you refuse to answer, the media, which monitors the police calls and covers all metro shootings, will note that the "shooter" is not cooperating with police. Guess where you are going?

After the humiliation of a formal booking at the county jail, complete with strip search, mug shot, fingerprints and one phone call, you get to sit it out with a diverse collection of cellmates, ranging from drunks, wife beaters, burglars, pimps and other folks who have found themselves in the same spot, awaiting unheeded pleas to relatives for bail or their first court appearance…next Tuesday.

Somewhere in all of this madness is the fact that you were defending your life against a violent armed robber who would have killed you in the process. But that is irrelevant right now because the only facts that the police have are the "witnesses" the one accomplice with vested amnesia, hostile "witnesses", and an "unarmed" corpse.

Fortunately, your desperate "one call" from jail was retrieved by your wife, three hours after the event as she frantically checked the voicemail from the home phone.

You called the home phone from jail because you were too emotionally distraught to even remember your wife's cell phone which she always answers, even when she is sitting for the neighbor's kids that night. The home phone is rarely used these days, but she finally discovered your jailhouse message in her panic to find out why you were not home by midnight.

You are innocent until proven guilty, but jailed until the judge sets bail.

Your wife races to jail to see you, but is greeted with the standard hand-out sheet with posted visiting hours, bail bond agencies phone numbers and a case number that she will need to reference when calling the police department which made the detention. Now, you are detainee # _____, not Bill Jones or Sam Smith, etc.

If you are lucky, you will get a private cell until your first hearing.

So, at 3 A.M. on Sunday morning, you are sitting in jail, awaiting potential charges of shooting an "unarmed" man. Your wife has contacted the police department, which advises that no information is available until the investigating officers file the preliminary paperwork. That preliminary report should be filed before end of shift at 7 A.M., just four hours away. Then she will just have a case number, cause for holding, pending preliminary charges and next scheduled visiting hours.

Even if he is your best friend, any attorney is not happy about your wife's hysterical call at 7:00 A.M. Sunday, especially regarding a potential self-defense/homicide call, involving you and an "unarmed" man.

If you are lucky, you will have a single cell. If not, you will develop a new understanding of the term "cellmates".

Your prescription medications will be delayed until confirmed by the jail doctor, who will be in Monday morning by 9 or 10 A.M....usually, unless he has an emergency call at the hospital, his full-time job.

Your attorney really looks forward to spending Sunday after church at the jail.

Early Sunday-morning phone calls from the jail are "welcomed" by your attorney.

Because he is your best friend and you do have standing in the community, a good job and a substantial investment portfolio, previously discussed with him during a financial planning appointment, he readily agrees to step in on your behalf. However, if you don't have all that going for you, the wait could be significantly longer and much more stressful as your "cellmates" attempt get to know you more intimately over time.

Even though your attorney's hourly fee is $350, Sunday morning activation of professional services does tend to stretch the bonds of friendship beyond normal expectations. Maybe, friendship will trump the usual Sunday premium hourly rate.

He will probably spend three to four hours on your behalf, obtaining the preliminary reports, pending charges, witness statements and visiting you in one of the starkly furnished jailhouse interview rooms. From there, he will contact your wife and explain the details and the challenges of your situation…and that he will follow-up with the matter at 9 A.M. Monday morning, a full day ahead of the first visiting-hours opportunity you will have with your wife for 10 minutes on Tuesday afternoon.

There is no scheduled bond amount for possible/pending murder charges. That is a matter that will be determined at the first court appearance.

Headlines will not be pleasant or kind…

Following the news reports, complete with your name, residence, place of employment, etc., all associated with shooting an unarmed man, your home will become a parade route for lots of gawkers, family and "associates" of the deceased and a host of media, wishing to interview your wife or any other family members.

Your employer will respond to your news by reassigning your duties, pending resolution of the case, and you will begin using what is left of your annual vacation time if you wish to continue receiving a paycheck…depending on your company's personnel policies…and that is the best-case probability.

In all likelihood, "innocent-until-proven-guilty" just doesn't help with your company's client relations or accounts. They will be reassigned and you will become corporately "non-existent".

The family will need to be relocated immediately.

Your wife and family, pets and all, will probably have to temporarily move in with relatives or stay in various undisclosed hotels until the situation quiets down or is resolved to the satisfaction of the decedent's family/ "associates"...and that could take a while.

Even your best relatives develop different "perspectives" for family visitors under the current circumstances, especially if they have your same last name and are listed in the phone book.

Isolation and not knowing what is going on to correct the matter are the toughest issues.

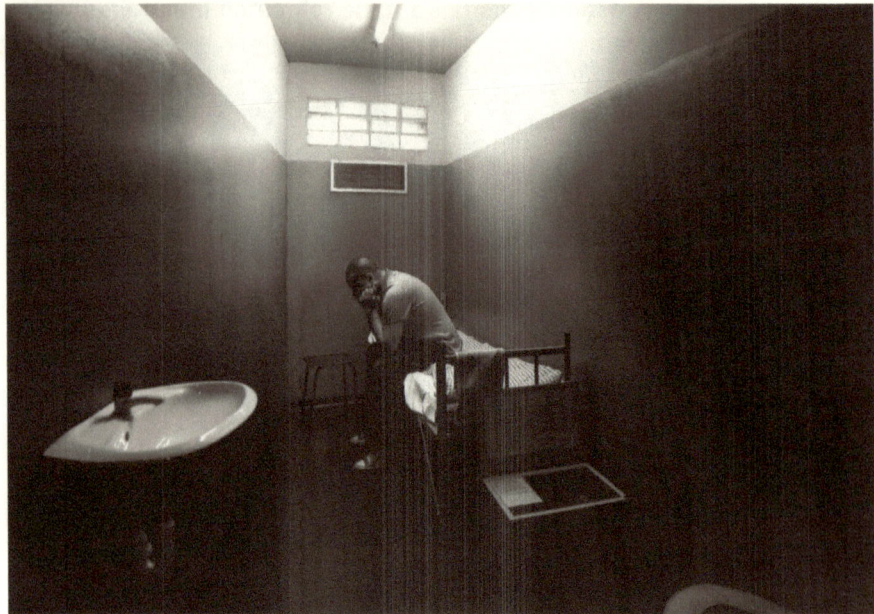

While the resolution process is going on, you are stuck in jail, branded as non-cooperative.

You are heeding the advice of your attorney to not discuss details until he has had sufficient time to review, speak with the prosecutor and subsequently sit beside you at your first court appearance, usually within three-five days after the incident.

Your wife will need to have the home guarded against vandalism, drive-by targeting or fire-bombing as revenge will motivate diverse retaliations.

You can do nothing but sit it out, hope for the best and add up what all of this is costing you…in dollars, reputation, career, family stress and danger…confident that "justice will prevail."

You feel certain that it will all be resolved, but the tab is going to be costly in every way, real dollars and other ways too.

The court is overloaded. You get five minutes for initial/bond hearing.

Your second court appearance goes much better.

Thanks to several witness statements from the gas station employees, your side of the story starts to receive some confirmation…but there is still no weapon from the alleged attacker. The judge assigns bail at $100,000, but you just have to put up 10% with a bail bond company to get out of jail five days later.

Saved by the Security Camera

Because the gas station security cameras were running at the time and captured the entire event on video, the prosecutor eventually decides to drop the case and all charges within just 10 days of the fatal event.

The bond is released and you are just out the attorney fees and 10% of the bond, total amount…$ 14,790 + 10-days hotel (family safety) $1200 + 24 hr. home watch $ 5,000 = $20,990…all because you defended yourself, lawfully, when someone tried to rob and kill you…but you survived and are still alive…just a few thousand dollars shy in your bank account, notwithstanding the future costs for post-traumatic-stress-disorder counselling and associated medications to get back to your normal self….but your wife and kids should be fine…So, you may not have any of those similar expenses to help them get back to normal also.

Your boss will probably let you back on the job, but it will never be the same…and you will need the money for the next chapter of your legal defense.

COURT OF THE SIXTH JUDICIAL DISTRICT OF THE
IN AND FOR THE COUNTY DISTRICT OF THE
MAGISTRATE DIVISION

Case No. CV-2014-253

LEGAL NOTICE

Court on the ....

Even though the police will not "buy" the attacker's associates' story, does not mean that an attorney for the family will not see an opportunity to pursue a civil action against you for some trumped-up accusation that you over reacted.

You will need a civil attorney to defend yourself against the evolutionary stories that will be crafted to paint you as the person in the wrong. It should not cost you more than $ 40,000-$75,000 additionally (about two weeks of attorney time for case preparations/depositions/trial/court costs) to defend yourself as you get to this point in the real-life scenario...and this is one of the better outcomes that can happen to you after your involvement in a shooting event.

If criminal charges were shown to have no basis and even if the civil case brought against you was found to be without merit, revenge of the dead party still lives in the relatives...in Federal Court. Violation of Civil Rights may very well be the next challenge you face as Federal charges can still be filed against you for depriving the individual of his "Civil Rights". It happens and defending yourself in Federal Court is very expensive, "noisy", usually involves defense team time, travel, lodging, and meals...tens of thousands of dollars, probably more like six figures.

The "Price of Freedom" is very high, even when you are innocent.

The bills mount up as you "prove your innocence".

And let's say that all goes well, you will probably have to sell your house (if it is still standing), find another job, move to another state or country, enroll the kids in a new school and always look over your shoulder because "revenge" never dies, especially the variety that is fueled by successive personal and legal setbacks on the part of robber's family.

And this is the condensed version of reality, mildly stated, just so you know the responsibilities, liabilities and consequences of legally carrying a defensive firearm and ever having to use it.   But at least you will be alive.

Chapter 17-What if you are at a restaurant...? It can't get worse...Yes it can !

You are sitting in a nice shopping mall food court with your family and a gunman enters to rob a restaurant. He points his gun at a terrified young cashier and demands money.

You, as a licensed gun carrying citizen realize that you could intervene and shoot at the robber, about 50 feet away from your table.

You draw, aim and shoot at the robber. You miss, but the sudden explosion from your gun scares the robber and he turns and runs out the door and disappears into the food-court crowd. Thinking you are the hero of the day, you rush over to the cashier and the line of people waiting to pay for their meal...only to discover...

The bullet missed the armed robber and hit an innocent patron.

That's when you notice that the bullet from your gun missed the robber, but it glanced off the wall and hit an innocent patron, standing five feet away from the register. He is bleeding severely from the bullet wound and people all around are panic-stricken from the retort of your gun, the blood and others, who did not see the robber, are screaming at you for shooting the person in line.

Good citizens may threaten to attack you and hold you down until the police arrive.

The cashier is so shaken that she cannot speak coherently and just points at you as she wails into a handful of paper napkins. Your family is scared and just wants to get away, but you can't leave, because you are the one who has "inflicted" injury on an innocent patron.

You can hear the ambulance siren, but it is far away, and he is bleeding.

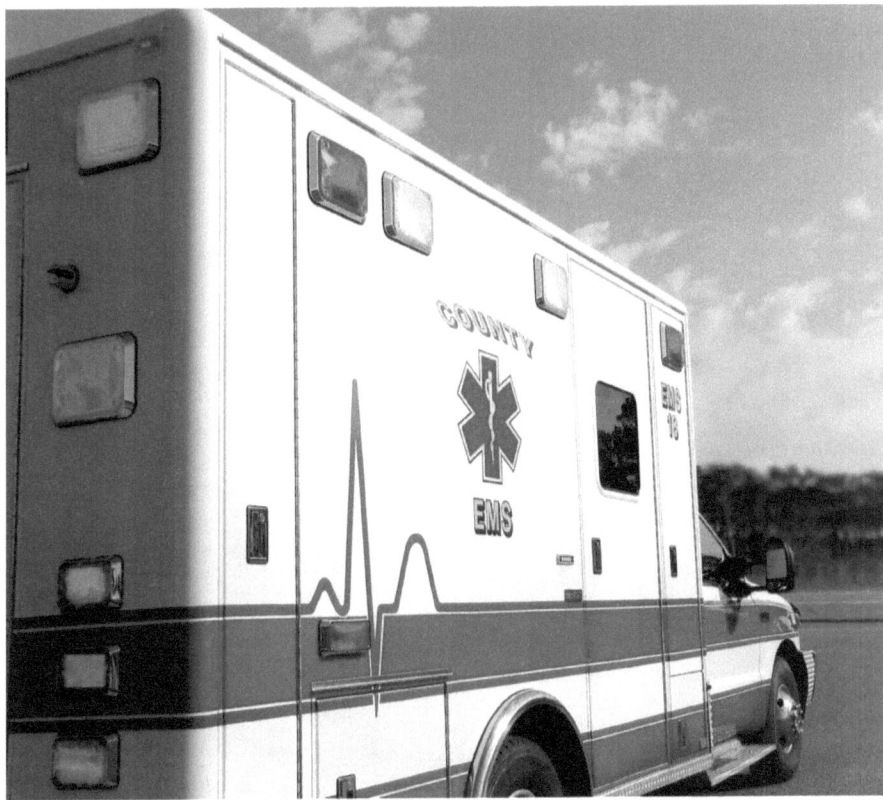

If you are lucky, there is a medical person in the crowd who steps in to help control the bleeding and tend to the injured person until the ambulance arrives...which seems like an eternity.

The first distant sirens you hear are from the police who have received 911 cell phone calls from other patrons that someone just shot someone and both parties are still in the restaurant.

911 Calls flood the police station & you are not the good guy in many of them.

Somehow the attempted robbery didn't get mentioned in the panic call to the police for help.

All they know is that someone is shot. They are bleeding all over the place and the guy who did it is wearing a green shirt and black pants, standing at the checkout counter…and still has the gun.

Guess who gets a gun in the face, a take down, full search, handcuffs and some serious treatment initially.

You can't blame them. They don't have the whole story yet, but they can't take any chances. So, you try to explain, but the guy with the serious wound has now slipped into unconsciousness because of blood loss.

Lots of chaos and emotion erupt until police secure the scene & record evidence/statements.

Your family tries to explain what happened, but the police have to secure the scene and separate the witnesses to process the evidence, but that is later....sometime after the ambulance arrives and takes the wounded person off to the hospital.

The officers will take your initial statement, probably while you are still handcuffed and escort you downtown, read you your rights and attempt to get the whole story from witnesses, most of whom have hastily left the scene because they don't want to get involved in a shooting investigation, have to go to court and miss work.

You have good support and legal teams…

Your outcome…good, but costly.

Your family will be left there in shock to relay details and ultimately contact an attorney at his home, arrange for a retainer fee and beg him to rush to the police station to help you with the situation.

If this is starting to sound familiar, it is because it is again the Reality 101 factor and Murphy's Law temporarily working against you until the facts show that you were innocent, and the situation was a total accident by a good citizen who was trying to protect everyone from a bad guy.

However, the story is a lot different at the hospital where some guy, trying to pay for his dinner, took a bullet and is fighting for survival…complete with all the emotions, concern and questions from his family and friends.

There is nothing you can do, but go along for the ride to the police station and possibly, the jail.

Back at the Hospital...

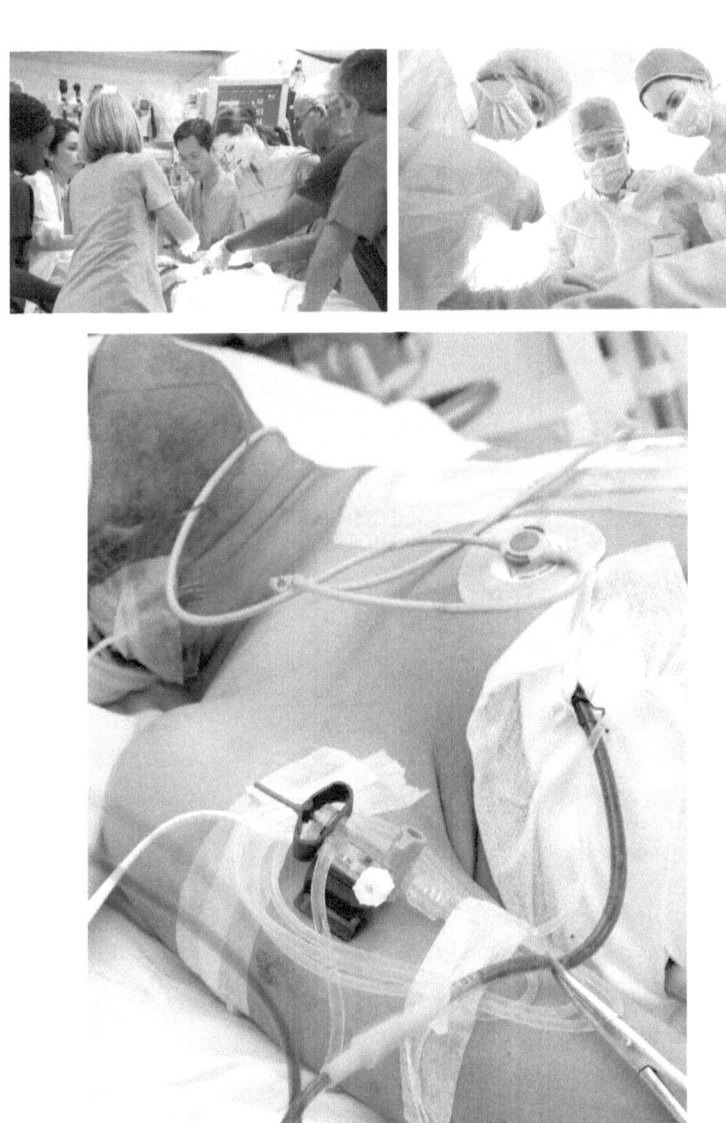

The wounded patron is on his third pint of blood transfusions and is still unconscious. Part of his family is at his side and some have showed up at the police station to talk to you.

Food court is back in business and wants everyone to forget...Not good for revenues.

Somehow the attempted robbery got lost in the confusion...in the food court.

The robber has escaped...It's just not good for business for the story to linger. What's even worse is that no one can even provide a description of the robber who started the madness. The franchisees are trying to forget the pool of blood at the front door and some guy struggling to breathe until the ambulance arrived.

Life picks up and goes on as usual, except for the guy in the hospital and you in the jail.

Your family calls to your attorney are eventually answered and responded to with the usual enthusiasm of a shooting call.

Finally, your attorney arrives at the police station and requests private time with you to review details, potential liabilities and next steps to clear your name and reputation.

The media will want to record your face and reaction for the story and file.

The media will already have an "attitude" about the shooting of an unarmed man.

You will have another opportunity to incriminate yourself.

The news media will certainly want to cover a local shooting in a public restaurant and the story will be "Breaking News" that night on the 11 P.M. edition, complete with your name, age, employment, city of residence.

However, since it is "Breaking News", they may not have all the details and will just report what they have been told, either by real or wannabe witnesses, seeking 30 seconds of no-fault fame on the local TV station…and what they say may not be accurate…for sure.

At home, the parade of cars will begin driving up and down your street, throwing things at your house. The phone will be ringing off the hook, Facebook, LinkedIn and Twitter will spark up with comments, most supportive, but many not. Some will be unkind, even hostile.

It's now about 3 A.M., seven hours after the attempted robbery that started the whole matter and the police have determined that you are not the robber; you tried to intervene; it all went wrong; someone is in the hospital with a severe wound from your gun, which is now in police custody also…for evidence….and the robber is gone, nowhere, drunk or asleep at home, celebrating and laughing for surviving another close call.

Your story checks out and you are out of jail, but not "out of the woods".

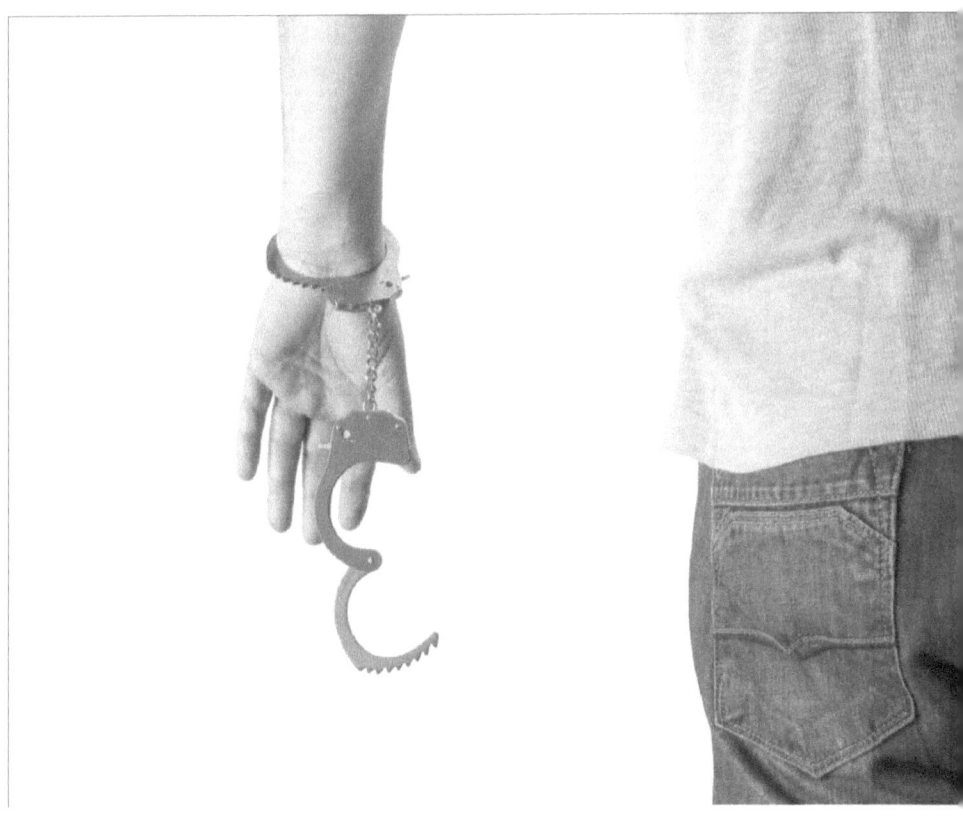

The police agree to release you at about 6 A.M., just ahead of shift change. Your wife meets you at the police station waiting room where she has been all night. Your attorney heads home with an appointment to meet you Monday afternoon to follow-up on the case. To this point, he has invested eight hours in your situation @ $350/hour.

And everyone who wasn't there has an opinion and attitude...

Later...the next afternoon, the parade of protesters will begin marching by your home.

The phone will be ringing off the hook, social media will spark up with comments, many supportive, but many not. Some will be unkind, even hostile...even threatening.

Back at the Hospital...

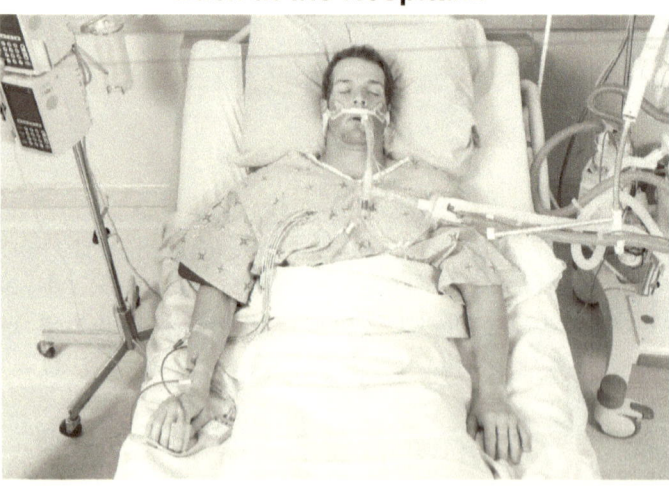

At the hospital, the injured person is still unconsciousness and his condition has been upgraded to "stable", which means nothing since HIPPA regulations prevent any other comment for his current condition.

A week later…

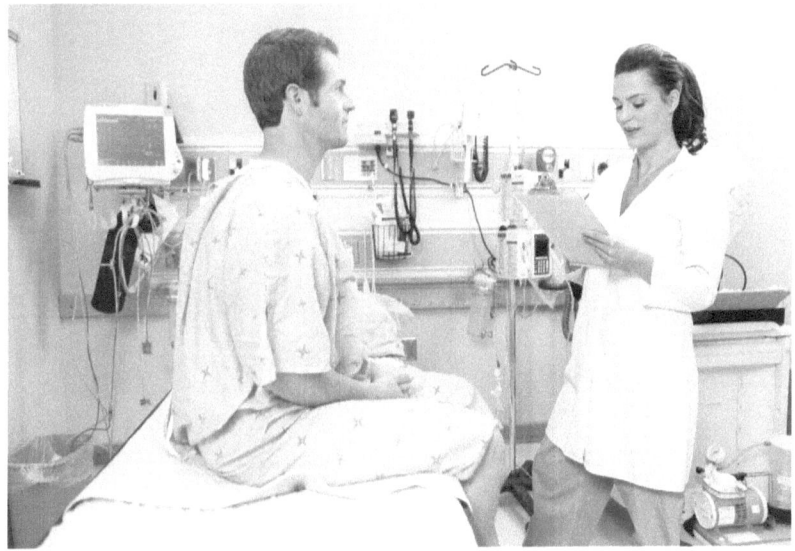

The victim is up and doing better and scheduled for release soon.

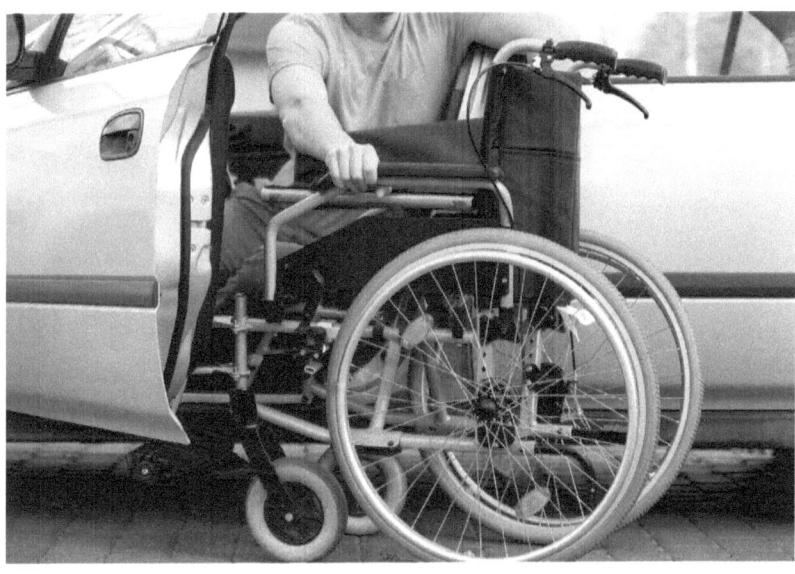

He is released ahead of schedule to recuperate and begin physical therapy at a local P.T. Center.

Released from the hospital, but not back to normal for the victim.

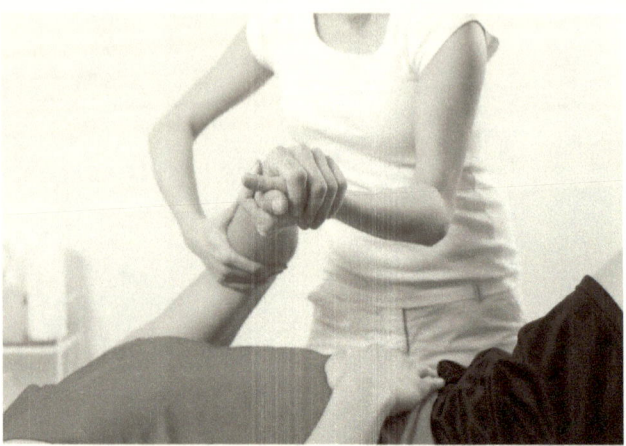

You can also expect a significant physical therapy, property remediation bills and employee counselling invoice from the restaurant owner, corporate office or legal department.

Back at work in a few weeks, he will eventually have a full recovery.

The wounded bystander will improve over the next five days and will be released to homecare where he will ultimately make a full recovery in six weeks and return to work in two months.

Cost for the ambulance, hospital stay, home care, and loss of two month's income tabs out at $74,574…and guess who will be contacted repeatedly or by a judgment until the financials are settled?

You will be spending a lot of time with your new legal team...

Your attorneys (You will need more than one.) advise that they will have to take preemptory depositions from witnesses and prepare formal defense for your impending civil lawsuit by the wounded patron.

Criminal charges for reckless use of handgun or some version of that are being reviewed by the county prosecutor's office, but adequate explanations, plus your agreement to cover all direct costs to the wounded patron will probably take any criminal charges off the table.

If you think all of these charges/costs are a small price to pay to still be alive...you are right, but it's still not over.

Again in this case, just because you faced no criminal charges, does not exclude the probability of a family member of the injured patron from seeking civil court liability against you for willful and negligent bodily injury.

The "scales of justice" swing on evidence and liability...

In a criminal case, the decision of guilt against you is held to the "beyond a reasonable doubt" standard, however in a civil case, liability is based on the "preponderance of evidence" against you...

...In other words, if it is 51% likely that you were wrong in your decision to use lethal force against the injured or deceased party, the court can issue a judgment against you for some unspecified amount of money, often...more than enough to bankrupt you and your family.

Contingency lawyers *(they get a cut of the judgment against you)* come out of the woodwork and line up for these opportunities. It is more likely to happen than not.

And don't forget the US Attorney General, who may again decide to be selectively righteous and seek Civil Rights investigation and charges against you, depending upon the circumstances and political pressure of the "mob justice seekers".

You have witnessed that "hot button", replayed more than once recently in the national media. You just don't want it played on you.

Your pre-carry meeting and discussion with your attorney reduces the chances that you will be the victim of an injustice agenda, political opportunists and mob panderers.

Chapter 18-Final Real-Life Story

Unmarked and Unknown Police Car

While working a plain-clothes detail in a new, at the time, Plymouth unmarked police car (which was not familiar yet by the other area police agencies), I was called to a family disturbance at a local residence, backup requested as a standard operating procedure.

Greeted at the door by the calling family member, I identified myself as a police officer and entered the residence to evaluate the situation. While I was leaning over a table to discuss the matter with one of the residents, seated in a chair, I heard a noise behind me, quickly turned around, only to be staring down the barrel of a .357 magnum revolver, pointed 12 inches from my nose.

It was just an instant, one of those "slow-motion" moments that occurs in a crisis situation and then…It was over as the deputy sheriff, responding to the back-up call, recognized me from my prior days on the sheriff's department reserve force and as a local police officer.

When he arrived at the scene, he did not recognize my brand new unmarked vehicle, and I was in plain clothes with my back turned to him as he entered the room.

The situation could have turned out tragically because he initially couldn't tell the "good guys from the bad guys"…and I was a police officer…What chance do you think you will have if you are involved in any gun incident to explain anything before you are cuffed, searched and escorted to the squad car for a subsequent conversation that will certainly be less than cordial, until the facts and players are sorted?

When you call 911 to report the incident, also tell the operator that you have a personal protection permit and are waiting for the police at __(location)____ and that your weapon is secured and holstered.

Chapter 19-What if...you make the best decision?

You are having a burger and Coke at a local bar and grille when one of the topics of NASCAR, NFL, NBA or the World Series comes up and the "well-imbibed" "room expert" proclaims that Dale Earnhardt was the best NASCAR driver in history, Michael Jordan the best basketball star or Peyton Manning the super football player of all time...whatever the topic and someone else disagrees. The "proclamations" escalate to an argument as others disagree, and then it all turns into a fight.

In fact, one of the "barstool commentators", somewhat "lubricated" by his fifth beer, looks your way and calls you a S.O.B. or whatever...and you are a wimp if you don't have anything to say about it...just to get your "participation" or involvement into the erupting altercation.

At that point, you remember rule #1...avoid situations, locations, events, people, geography that can lead to violence.

You just "drop" a cash on the tab, tip included, no-receipt-needed and leave, even though you have been characterized by non-glowing adjectives or insults.

Pay the tab, tip, count your blessings and leave…

The gun does not license you to settle or resolve idiot-level disagreements that have gotten out of hand. That is why the police, 911 and cell phones, and the nearest exit doors exist.

You can't win an argument with idiots on alcohol because they will overwhelm you on two counts…idiot and alcohol.

No liability here, except for the food/drink tab. (Note: In some states, municipalities, it is illegal to carry a gun while visiting a bar or establishment that serves alcohol.) Count your blessings and remember rule #1 and all that it has saved you. You now have one more place to avoid on your list.

Chapter 20-What if the real-life nightmare happens to you?

It really happened...You have been attacked...Life-threatening, violent attack...and you defended your life with lethal force.

O.K., now that you have defended yourself from a life-or-death attack by an armed thug by discharging your firearm and wounding/killing the attacker, the life-challenging threats covered previously are just beginning for you, starting with the many forces that will begin to "play" on you, internally and externally. Sounds like a re-run of the same movie...but this time it's personal.

You may be injured yourself from the altercation, cut, wounded, bleeding and need immediate medical attention. Be sure to ask for it. Second, you will probably be in shock or reacting to adrenalin that may cause you to become sick, faint or pass out. You have never experienced the feeling of a life-death encounter that required you to stop the aggression with lethal force.

You may even experience a surreal or slow-motion view of the immediate moments surrounding the event...during and after. However, your future survival will depend upon how well you cope with those natural responses and deal with the "load of emotions" and all the related issues that will be thrust upon you.

First, make sure that the threat is really neutralized and that any weapon associated with the attacker is no longer available to him, either by moving it a safe distance away or by removing it to a safe place...out of the reach, not only the attacker, but also his friends, relatives, sympathizers or other opportunists, who will naturally gravitate to the scene after the sound of gunfire and the screams of "a man shot."

Remember, your first duty is to protect yourself from any subsequent or secondary threats associated with the incident. That means, assure yourself that the threat will not re-energize, that others may not take up the aggressor's cause and that you preserve the immediate and subsequent moments with your cell phone camera, right as you call 911 for assistance.

Get the scene picture/video & call the police.

You must do this within the first few seconds or within the first minute of the shooting. Otherwise, you have lost the moment and most likely your chance at legal self-defense and a future "normal" life. Some "Do Gooders" will criticize this sequence by saying that you should render first aid to the assailant and try to save his life until the ambulance arrives.

These same Monday-morning "Do Gooders" cannot be certain that the attacker is totally incapacitated and not capable of fulfilling his original intent…to kill you? Can they answer the question of whether he has another gun, knife or other potentially lethal weapon on his person, in his pocket or hidden, but still available to him?

The "gang" might decide to help their downed "dude"…

"Associates" may be suddenly motivated to avenge his demise and lunge at you while you are attempting to administer aid.

You responded initially out of grave fear to protect your life and it is still in danger until the police arrive and secure the scene. First aid can kill you if you are not aware of how it can "backfire" on you. Ultimately, you must make your own decision, based upon the particular situation and circumstances…another topic you should discuss with your attorney as part of your responsibility before even thinking of carrying a weapon.

Others may want to rush to his aid and start screaming at you for being so heartless.

If you let someone "tend" to the wounded/dead attacker, you run the risk of even higher emotions once they determine that he is dead or the "caregivers" may use the crisis to remove more evidence, weapons, drugs, loot, and/or personal belongings of the attacker. There is nothing like a tragedy to bring out the opportunists. It's a tough call, but you have to assess the crowd and determine the risks of the moment if you let a crowd-stranger enter the crime scene area.

Make sure that your gun is back in your holster, pocket, wherever…out of sight to onlookers. The longer you keep it on display, the more likely there are to be more misinterpretations of your intentions and who was at fault in their minds.

Remember, "the onlookers" probably didn't see what happened, just came on the scene after the shot(s), only to see you with the gun and that somebody has been shot. They don't know the lead-up story, but will come up with one on their own if they continue to see you flashing a gun in your hand.

Someone might even view you as the aggressor and decide to "protect themselves" by shooting you…just to "save" everyone gathered. The story changes by the second when emotions start to drive the story as we have seen so many times in the media recently.

Your 911 call to police/ambulance will be just one of many from various parties related to this incident, and you can bet that some of the other callers will describe you as the man with the gun who shot somebody.

Knowing that fact, your call should be made as soon as possible and include the fact that you were attacked and feared for your life when you were forced to defend your life. He is injured, but you are afraid to go near him…and you may be injured too. State that your gun is holstered/secure and you are waiting for assistance by the police and medical personnel are needed to help as quickly as possible at ___ (location) ___. "Please send help. Thank you."

You can leave you phone number, but the 911 operator probably already has it from your caller I.D. If you are in a position to answer the inevitable return call from the 911 operator, just confirm the location and that you need the police and an ambulance. To answer any other questions will just create another opportunity for you to say something, that will be recorded, and played back to you by the prosecutor if you are charged criminally or the plaintiff's lawyer in a civil lawsuit, which will generally follow, unless you have several still-present, pristine witnesses to the entire event, video of the actual attack and response and/or photos of the crime scene. Hopefully the attacker's rap sheet clearly indicates a career violent criminal background and no surviving family members (who could use a few extra hundreds of thousands of dollars from a judgement against you).

Again, the standard for convicting you of murder/manslaughter/ felonious assault requires a "beyond a reasonable doubt" level of jury confidence to send you away for killing another person. However, a civil suit against you only requires "preponderance of the evidence", meaning that if it is 51% more likely that you were in the wrong in using deadly force to prevent the attack against you, then a jury/judge can award damages to the plaintiff or plaintiff's family if he is deceased and that judgement dollar amount against you can be 5, 6, or 7 figures.

The justice system is as fair as the evidence supports.

A judgement can attach to your bank account, savings, IRA, wages, other income until the balance is paid....and everyone is motivated to go for it, especially the attorney, who gets a big percentage of the take.

Proving your innocence can be expensive, but the alternatives are much worse.

Your survival can cost you everything, unless you protect yourself from all threats.

COURT OF THE SIXTH JUDICIAL DISTRICT OF THE

IN AND FOR THE COUNTY

MAGISTRATE DIVISION

Case No. CV-2014-253

LEGAL NOTICE

Court on the ....

What is the right direction...?

The decision is yours, the choices are yours, the responsibility is yours...and most importantly, the life is yours...and that makes everything else worth it.

These real-life accounts, scenarios and examples are not provided to discourage you from legally possessing and carrying (with a proper license) a firearm for your self-defense. Part of the responsibility that goes along with that Constitutional Right is to understand all the ramifications that go along with it.

Liability on many levels is just part of that overall recognition and responsibility. Additionally, training, practice, safety, awareness and predetermination of the lawful rules of engagement must accompany your decision and ongoing plan for reasonable and rational self-defense associated with carrying a firearm.

Whichever of these scenarios and any of a thousand others, you may hopefully never encounter, there are some universal points that you should always consider and act upon.

How would you feel if you left your gun and permit at home and you and your family fell under the gun of a crazed criminal or terrorist? It's all over in seconds. You just have to be aware, ready and committed to whatever it takes to keep yourself and your family safe from the madness and the people who think nothing of killing you and everyone around you to get what they want or to pursue a misguided, demented agenda.

Evaluate your <u>total</u> personal protection plan...

According to United States Concealed Carry Association, a leading provider of training, membership insurance and research, 97% of all drivers in the United States have vehicle, medical and liability insurance, but only 3% of the licensed gun permit citizens have liability coverage for their self-defense...97% have no liability, expense, bond, or legal defense coverage.

A shocking statistic from the United States Concealed Carry Association

"97% of all drivers in the United States have vehicle, medical and liability insurance but only 3% of the licensed gun permit citizens have liability coverage for their self-defense..."

Chapter 21-Concealed Carry "CYA" (Cover Your Ass...ets.)

The best way to prepare for the realities of defending yourself against a life-threatening attack and subsequent financial challenges associated with it, is to responsibly arm yourself all the way around...with an informed-choice weapon, state license to carry, safety training, range practice, self-defense training, a lawyer conference, bail bond insurance and legal defense insurance as well as written detailed instructions to a reliable/available contact or family member for the one call you are entitled to make from the jail/police station...to begin the legal defense process after your involvement in a self-defense gun event.

If you don't plan for the contingencies, you may become the victim of all that can go wrong...Just recall the recent news coverage of citizens and police officers who have used legally-justified lethal force to defend themselves or someone else. Innocence and justification on your part have no bearing on the "mob mentality" fueled by hate groups or political opportunists, both seeking to advance their cause or office or election to office.

Just as you wouldn't get behind the wheel of a car without license plates, drivers manual/training, insurance, don't even think of carrying a gun or "getting behind the trigger" without installing the same degree of comprehensive "CYA" measures.

You can survive a potentially lethal attack and the subsequent financial ones by completing your plan now, before it is too late, too expensive, or worse, fatal to you or a loved one.

Now that you have completed the book, Concealed Carry "CYA", the next step is to protect yourself with membership/insurance to cover the *Murphy's Law* factors that always emerge. Don't even think of carrying a gun until you do.

When you first noticed the cover of this book, the sub-title no longer applies to you and has now changed:

What you do know can ***save*** you everything!

In addition to the training, experience and vigilance, I personally signed up a couple of years ago for invaluable legal/financial insurance that covers many of the major expenses associated with a self-defense incident.

(Your homeowner's policy will not even begin to CYA on these issues.)

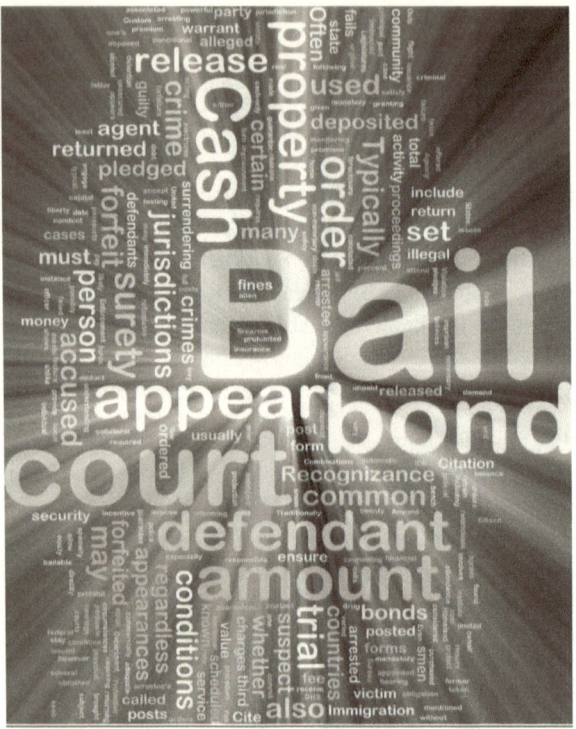

The membership covers bail bond, a criminal defense fund and civil defense fund. Additionally, it offers a significant level of coverage and a vital part of the responsibility associated with my carrying a personal protection handgun. It is very affordable with a choice of small monthly payments, depending upon the level of coverage you select, but it's worth every penny…just for the peace of mind…a small price for a huge benefit.

Thank you for reading and best of safekeeping and good fortune to you and your family. You can get more information about this valuable resource and protection on the accompanying website **www.ConcealedCarryCYA.com**

John F. Pyzik

www.ConcealedCarryCYA.com

www.ingramcontent.com/pod-product-compliance
Lightning Source LLC
Chambersburg PA
CBHW030344290526
45785CB00004B/1588